find her.
keep her.

find her,
keep her.

Renaada Williams

Andrews McMeel
PUBLISHING®

trigger warning

dear beautiful reader . . .

i deeply appreciate you embarking on this journey with me, but before we continue, let's check in.

i know a lot of you are tuned in because you genuinely enjoy my work, and some of you are here because we've gone through similar journeys. i'd like us first to take a deep breath and check in with ourselves, and ask questions like how do you feel? what mental space are you in right now? do you feel okay enough to read through something that may trigger any unwanted feelings or emotions?

i'd like you to take this time to be completely honest with yourself, and if you cannot handle it, i will never take any offense to you taking care of your mental health . . .

trust me, i'll still be here!

for everyone else, i'd like us to take another deep breath and understand this book contains the following triggers. (i've listed page numbers as well in the event you'd simply prefer to skip over them.)

1. self-harm: 16, 37
2. racism: "two americas" chapter
3. sexual assault: 88, 89, 92
4. trauma
5. child abuse: 58, 80, 87
& possibly more.

remember to always take care of yourself.

i love you.

significance

take my hand . . . as we journey back home.
together

searching.

i spent a lot of time
searching
looking for myself
in everything i did
in everyone i had
or those
who've had me
spent a lot of time
not understanding
the longer it took
to find my way back
home
the greater the loss
would be.

"finders keepers"

how ironic is it
to settle
abandon my identity
starve with distaste
and ultimately be forced
to learn from lessons
i taught.

find her. keep her.

i didn't want to write about another heartbreak

you looked at me
with eyes that said
you'd never love again
but i grabbed your hand
knowingly
risking it all

- forever went by quickly

i thought i was ready
until my body froze
because you smelled familiar
like heartache
dipped in your favorite cologne

you talked as if the spread was full
as if there would be a plethora of things
i would receive
like i'd never get full
like i'd always have seconds
you talked as if
you took the time
for *preparation*
as if you knew exactly what i wanted like
you were confident i'd have it
and i'm sure at one point you did
i'm sure you had everything i ever wanted
i'm certain i would've been fulfilled
if i had known how long it took
if i had gotten here sooner
if i hadn't been preparing myself as well
taken the time to get *me* ready
maybe i would've gotten more
than just scraps.

it's possible
to want something you've never known
something you haven't felt
to wonder how it tastes
it's possible to fall in love
with *dreaming.*

i thought i finally had
love that loved me back
and it made
everything
forgivable

you saw me
measured me up
mustered up enough
representation
for my cravings
i filled you up
enough to survive endless winters
enough to rid yourself of the mask
enough to be you
you enough
to never desire me again.

some of me wants
to want
nothing to do with you
and most of me
still wants you to call

so determined to prove not everyone
gives up
not everyone leaves
so determined
to stay
just to be left
here with me
anyway

and if all i had to give
was the effort of trying
that's enough for me.

i don't want something else to remind you that i exist

- second thought

i need you to get to know me
before she comes
i need you to talk to me
to hold me
to kiss me
to tell me that it will be okay
when she gets here
i need you to promise me love
even if she forces your hand
i need to know that you'll stay
with the both of us

- bipolar

she told me i was
easier to love when i was happy
maybe before i felt alone
before all the arguments
before the infidelity
before all the times i questioned myself
and my sanity
maybe i should've eaten it
maybe i should have rinsed away my feelings
with the blood
maybe my body and my heart
could've healed
together.

you send music like apology
cuz' lyrics be spittin'
and if you never knew anything else
you know i'll always listen.

knowing you're no good for me
is like a slow burn
i crave the unknown
anticipate the pleasure
but i always
expect the pain.

love you like
drive to you
clean for you
cook for you
sing to you
nurture you
release with you
and still never be
enough for you.

i thought it was
impossible
to love me and have someone else
but you managed to screw us both
and still come out
smiling.

tell me
that love would
never be the same after me
and proceed to give her
everything

i wonder what it's like
not letting the
sugar settle
to crave sweetness so badly
you mix flavors
when you speak.

if i tell you
i love you
it means i accept the way you treat me
and
i
don't.

find her. keep her.

there is love in my heart
buried underneath strength
tucked in
weary
i can feel you trying to navigate through
compass

if i am
too much to handle
surrender the load.
release

find me when you're ready
so that love
can finally stay

- life partner

please
please understand that i want nothing
more than to have someone who
means it
someone who'll stay
even after they see
the unrecognizable parts in me
the parts they thought should
shimmer
the me behind all this light
the girl that may just
flicker
please understand that
i am terrified
not guarded
i am not afraid of what can happen
but i feel like i will shatter if nothing does so
please
tell me anything
tell me that i am beautiful
tell me that you trust me
tell me i'm important
affirm my feelings are valid
say any- and everything but this
cuz' i'd rather die alone
than bear a lifetime of false bliss.
i love you

i'm starting to feel like love
is only in fairy tales after all
however
i believe in magic.

records of self-discovery

i am not strong
i am fragile
i am emotional
i am sensitive
i am intense
i am well-dressed bone
covered in flesh
i am years of forgiveness
most times without apology
i am tender
i am a journey
that did not turn me cold
so please
be gentle with me.

i am not meant to be fixed
there isn't anything *broken* about me

i've spent years
laying bricks
doubling up on armor
preparing myself for war
or happiness
because both of them
have the ability to take me by surprise
to make me feel
less protected
to convince myself that as soon as i have either
they'll always switch places and then back again
it'll always be someone or something willing to risk it all
or give it all
just to take it back again
i've spent years convincing myself that i can handle it
that i can weather the storm
that i can be both soldier and pacifist

they treat
weakness
like a death sentence
like once you fall
you lose the ability to rise
like strength be easy
knowing it's rare
to have one without the other.

they say better days are coming
but they never tell you when
they want you to be resilient
make sure you have the toughest skin
i prayed for "okay" days for life
and it never changed a thing
i got better at hiding the scars
a hopeless dove without her wings

don't believe
anything or anyone
making you feel unworthy
even if it's yourself!

- check in

pick her up
wipe her face
pour into her
tell her
it's going to be okay
we deserve more
let her know you'll
always have her back.

- inner child work

passing me on the street is like
crying myself to sleep the night before
not wanting to wake up that morning
going to work laughing and joking long enough
for people not to ask me any questions
like
forgetting to listen to my stomach
because all i hear are my thoughts
not
crashing my car
being responsible for everyone on the road
i am not okay
i still remembered to send my "good morning" texts though
still reaching out to people
that cannot sense me
feel me
i shaved my legs and that's all i did with the razor today
i didn't take any medicine with fear
that i'd take more than the pain away
i was in so
much
pain today
so passing me on the street today while calling me
beautiful damn

ain't i though?

find her. keep her.

random gazes
stomach-clenching laughter
vows of forever
impromptu dance battles
endless karaoke
freestyle songs
undivided attention
gentleness
grace

- worth it

no alcohol
no drugs
i didn't really have any vices
i've had to deal
and heal myself
sober
since i've met me.

i am getting comfortable with the realization that i'm not always right.

i am
constantly
reminding myself
in order to move on
i had to actually
get up.

- volume

remember how we talked about survival?
and how we would fight
even if our body couldn't take it anymore?
i knew you could do it!
i knew you could choose *us* and see me waiting
     for you here . . .
i'm sorry if you still feel lost sometimes.
i'm sorry if i seem to be more hateful than grateful.
sometimes i still don't have the answers,
but i always have the faith!
so even though we have a long way to go,
just know . . .
i promise to protect you.
i promise to listen when you speak.
i promise to never take you for granted.
i promise to keep the light in me.
i promise you will be fulfilled
if it's the last thing i do,
and if i die before i save you,
know that i'm coming back for you.

P.S. you are a warrior; trust your power!

return me back
to my smile
my laugh
swap out the intensity in my eyes
for sparkle
for tender
lead me back
to my body
even if i have to claw my way in
even if that flesh don't fit
help me find my way back
to my heart
even if the rhythm's missing
even if it's too frail to touch
even if it's just beat'n

- home

tree folk

they say
home is where the heart is
but
here i am
holding on to scattered pieces
hoping it'd be enough
for shelter.

growing up learnin'
everybody's business
ain't nobody's business
meant to
cover your mouth for the family
smile in public
only speak good things
protect
the pedophile
the abuser
the rapist
the narcissist
convenient Christians
lie if you have to
seek help
but only share your part
try to keep afloat
drown
they'll say you were pushed anyway
cuz' our business
ain't nobody's
god damn business.

- tree folk

surround yourself with people
who can interpret your silence
rather than those
who come around
and can barely understand you
when you speak.

breaking branches
like
it ain't taking
life
away from you
like
you could survive
without them.

- *mature*

find her. keep her.

maybe
if you look long enough
you can see the beauty
in the damage
not the *brokenness*

i hate that
you only seem excited
when it's beneficial
when it's time
to claim things like
good parenting
home training
me
i hate that
you seem to love me more
now that the world can hear me speak
you're trying to
love me into silence
stuff my voice with memories
of a person you try on
when i know what's underneath.

phase be like
question me
confuse me
abandon me
choose me
impersonate me
abuse me
take me
control me
fuck me
mold me phase
be like not.

leave
build a new life
right in front of my eyes
father unrelated children
neglecting your own
teaching my first lesson
showing me
i can come from
someone
and still
be left alone
setting the tone to seek

love
even through
abandonment.

- teacher's pet

i am tired of trying to be
happy enough
for everybody else.

the roots have been
sanctioned
to break through the soil
watch them sprout
everywhere
allow it to take up
as much space as it needs
repot if necessary
never let it wilt
just to stay somewhere that
no longer feels like home.

find her. keep her.

sometimes
i feel like my friends and family
are tired of my sadness . . .
those days i just try a little harder to
choose to *survive.*

blood be like
taunt me
neglect me
play me
abandon me
lie for me
fuck me
haunt me
ignore me
protect me
control me
forgive me

- a slow drip

they tell me that i am difficult
too emotional
they say i need to find a better passion
one that just brings in the money
and doesn't tell their secrets
they tell me that i am sad
as if i am not myself
as if conversations were only had
after they got here

- tag, you're it.

he called
came in apology spoken
vulnerability reeking
without the need
or desire
for feedback
acknowledging wounds
i was made to believe were
self-inflicted
trauma only a distant father
could recognize
and begin to heal in one breath.

- apologies from my father

find her. keep her.

i send wishes like
tight palms
with shut eyes
drowning sound out
to let *grams* fall
like boulders
releasing every bit of me
with desire.

- well

two americas

blood splattered
painted on every branch
of our family tree
thunderstorms
thicker than
saws to set me free

they welcome me
my magic
my light
they say
i am
a gift
a token
they welcomed me
my laughter
my entertainment
my pain
my movement
but ask me
to leave my roots
at the door.

- conditional seats

we be
parent
athlete
teacher
lawyer
doctor
rapper
singer
dancer
poet
creator
actor
actress
God
and still
Nigga.

must be nice
to try on our skin
and fill your gaps with our reality

cold enough to be sick
Black enough for the risk
remove the hood
the hat
the gloves
we don't have
the luxury of warmth
Black enough
to be mistaken
for thief
for killer
for perp
Black enough to be everything
but happy
but child
but scared
Black enough to be everything but
human.

- winter days

we are out here
fighting for our lives
just to be killed anyway.

i don't
have to hold your hand
i don't
have to feed you
accessible
news or information
i don't
have to give grace
where i feel there is none
for me
an ally
by my definition
shows up
with
or without me.

if you're
more upset
about the fact that i keep
writing about my reality
than helping me change it you
become part of the problem.

find her. keep her.

they call us everything but soft
but delicate
as if our skin ain't butter
as if our Black ain't sweet
like grace come easy
like freedom is free

sun-danced
into the day
praying that *mon*day
would be better
*tues*day i arrived
broken
*wed*nesday's gonna allow us
to feel *human* again
*thurs*day feeling like
my body's given up
free . . . i mean *fri*day ain't so sweet here
*sat*urdays but Black be
resilient.

- the weak isn't Black

nobody *ever*
stencils a rainbow
and thinks
how beautiful it would be
without color.
and still

if
love is love
why ain't it?

Black be pure. Black be joy. Black be scared. Black be
laughter. Black be struggle. Black be happiness. Black be
journey. Black be lonely. Black be gold. Black be painful.
Black be beautiful. Black be healing. Black be restless. Black
be guarded. Black be radical. Black be love. Black be honest.
Black be talented. Black be hope. Black be stolen. Black
be sacred. Black be magic. Black be worthy. Black be
powerful. Black be passionate. Black be peace. Black be
fruitful. Black be home. Black be tryna' be broken.

Black be resilient.
Black be resilient.
Black be resilient.
Black be resilient.
Black be resilient.
Black be resilient.
Black be resilient.
Black be resilient.
Black be resilient.
Black be resilient.
Black be resilient.
Black be resilient.
Black be resilient.
Black be resilient.
Black be resilient.
Black be resilient.
Black be resilient.
Black be resilient.
Black be resilient.
Black be resilient.

Black be resilient.
Black be resilient.
Black be resilient.
Black be resilient.
Black be resilient.
Black be resilient.
Black be resilient.
Black be resilient.
Black be resilient.
Black be resilient.
Black be resilient.
Black be resilient.
Black be resilient.
Black be resilient.
Black be resilient.
Black be resilient.
Black be resilient.
Black be resilient.
Black be resilient.
Black be resilient.
Black be resilient.
Black be resilient.

snatch

i was still trying to figure out
what it was
and all that it could do
but you took it
before i even knew what to do with it

- snatched

wrapped up in the smoke
too much rage to be high
watch me
look me in the eyes
i watch you
i watch as you trace the outline of my body
up to my face
lock in my eyes
and still feel nothing

- ego

the glow in your eyes is
frightening

you asked me
to *forget*
like
past ain't present
like
trust ain't pending
like
hearts ain't mending.

i trace my body
trying to find the places
that feel good
the places that are safe
to touch
to caress
trying to find the places
that can exist without memory
the spots i can share
without triggering

she be
ready
or so she thinks
tight enough
for pleasure
strong enough
to sink.

i wonder
what it's like
to trust someone enough to climax.

i thought i had escaped
thought my day-mares were over
thought it'd be good
to have a friend
to *play* with
until the playing
never stopped
until the playing
was no longer fun
pretend daddy more present
than my father ever was
but at least
i had a home
i could depend on.

my first kiss on flesh
was nothing i'd imagine
i played pretend so long i wish i could go back

- running away from home into a graveyard

i never liked dresses
never liked the way they made me feel
more *accessible* than delicate
how some ignored the fact that
i was supposed
to keep my legs closed
i mean crossed
when wearing it
how it made me feel like
i was free
how painful it was to discover
i actually couldn't fly
how pretty *they* said i looked
how it granted consent
before i did
how the attention was tunneled
how it received more check ups
than i ever have
how it dressed up my sorrow
how it made me disappear.

- curtsy

find her. keep her.

my story feels like adrenaline
like challenge
like what if i could fix it

i felt like i needed permission
to touch myself
to make me feel good
to feel more satisfaction than pain
to take control back
to know that it's mine
i felt like i needed to ask
if it was okay to please me.

take me
closed eyes
take me
dark room
take me
half-clothed
take me
soundless
love me
love me
comfort
love me
gentle
love me
passionate
love me back
into myself

love
me

love
me

așé

find her. keep her.

i am constantly working on the person my inner child
needs me to become.

i
have to take
responsibility
over my heart
over my spirit
over myself.

find her. keep her.

rest
buy yourself some flowers
light a candle
dance
sing
release
release
release

you
have the ability
to create your reality.

the part of you
that feels like
or keeps telling you that
you cannot do it
is lying.

i love myself more
when i'm being honest
honest about what i like
honest about things i don't

complain
all you want
so long as it
renders some
solutions.

i have the ability to rebirth as many times as i see fit.

i am
beautiful
empathetic
caring
loving
trustworthy
i am
a force to be reckoned with.

- notes to self

self-care
is also
screaming
sleeping
crying
watching tv
and
maybe even
throwing things.

find her. keep her.

it's okay if you want to start
tomorrow.

- gentle reminders

i am grateful for life
i am grateful for mercy
i am grateful for my lessons
i am grateful for my health
i am grateful for creativity
i am grateful for peace
i am grateful for joy
i am grateful
i am grateful
i am grateful
i am grateful
i am grateful
i am grateful
i am grateful
i am grateful
i am grateful
i am grateful
i am grateful

i am a combination
of beautiful sunsets
and never-ending rivers.

take a deep breath
place your hand over your heart
create space
give yourself grace

love is always going to feel however you say it will because there's power in your tongue.

i dance in the mirror
prancing around holding my belly
i'm saying goodbye to my stomach
for it will no longer look this way again.
i sing into the morning
eating oatmeal and trail mix together
unable to curb my growing appetite
realizing that change happens
ever so swiftly
i cry into the night
hunched over
pain piercing through a flutter-less tummy
and a very weary back.
i met you at my sanctuary
chilled floors tiptoeing back into my memory
you flow like a river
twirling around into the distance
leaving nothing but dirty laundry
and me
alone
all over again.

- uproot

i held my breath
listened to your heartbeat
now i know
i have the ability
to create *home*
inside of me.

home be like
comfort
safety
good energy
honesty
home-cooked meals
losing myself
and
finding me again
cozy
memories
protection
love

find her. keep her.

home is wherever the fuck i say it is
but mostly
within myself

find her. keep her.

Andrews McMeel Publishing
a division of Andrews McMeel Universal
1130 Walnut Street, Kansas City, Missouri 64106

www.andrewsmcmeel.com

22 23 24 25 26 VEP 10 9 8 7 6 5 4 3 2 1

ISBN: 978-1-5248-7390-5

Library of Congress Control Number: 2022937556

Editor: Patty Rice
Art Director: Tiffany Meairs
Production Editor: Meg Utz
Production Manager: Julie Skalla

Cover and interior illustrations by Justin Estcourt

ATTENTION: SCHOOLS AND BUSINESSES
Andrews McMeel books are available at quantity discounts with bulk purchase for educational, business, or sales promotional use. For information, please e-mail the Andrews McMeel Publishing Special Sales Department: specialsales@amuniversal.com.